Dynamic minds

Jane Aguiar

Presentation by *BookLeaf Publishing*

Web: www.bookleafpub.com

E-mail: info@bookleafpub.com

ISBN:9789358311013

First edition 2023

DEDICATION

To

Mom and Dad

ACKNOWLEDGEMENT

"I start by being grateful to my parents for providing me with education and encouraging me to convey my feelings."

"I Thank my Husband for understanding me all the time. I also thank my daughter for motivating me.

"I sincerely thank bookleafpublishing.freshdesk.com for #ThewriteAngle Writing Challenge and for giving me the opportunity of publishing a book."

PREFACE

Being a Science student I developed an interest in Literature. I have completed my Bachelor in Science and Bachelor in Education. I am a working woman now who started poetry as a hobby. I have been writing syllabic poetic forms, free verse poetry, poetry prose, hymns, rhymes and flash fiction. Each poem of mine is a silvery white silk feather. I write my creations, perspectives, imaginations, feelings, emotions and muses thoughts. I got inspired by my other friends who are poets. Writing poetry built my confidence and helped me to learn a lot of new things. After gaining so much experience and confidence I took a step forward by publishing this book. I wish to have a book by my name in the libraries. All the poetries in this book include our feelings and emotions revealing the little fights between our heart and mind. Also, these poem forms are easy to learn. My poems may help not only youngsters but also people of all age groups to learn more about these poetry forms. I believe that poetry also works as a medicine for people in pain, it inspires people.

Trampled flower

Complete
transformation
of a trampled flower
recharge the system with
new pain of hope
and faith

Brain runs
like a metro
it does not like to bear
stress, but it has to bear
hardships given
by love

Form: Badger's Hexastitch

Love's life

You are
a beautiful
gentle and delicate vine
that blooms gracefully in the yard.
A string
of clear rainbow dreams that balances
accompanies my dream
on the path of
love's life.

Form: Butterfly Cinquain

To fetch love

As your arms are outstretched
My darkness will end
Long dark nights are wretched
You are a Godsend

You are a Godsend
And deep inside I've sketched.
You my dearest friend
And without you I'm stretched

And without you I'm stretched
I think we depend
On each other to fetch
Love, we both intend

Form: Chain verse as a crown

Souls of distant world

Souls of distant world
peeked into the depths of eyes
love's stimulated.
Butterflies in my stomach
mind shows nervousness
that turns the world upside down.
A great happiness
mind,soul,heart and body feels
the sense of experience.

Form: Choka

Cursed lover

The clouds
swelled and the rain
fell as if the clouds bath
the earth with love which is a long
scandal

Beneath
the beautiful
painted sky a long blaze
Is eager to meet his cursed
lover

Crapsey Cinquain

Fingers Intertwined

You and I
always want
to brighten our lives and hope for
the progress and blessings of all.
May God fulfil our wishes on time.

I want to
feel you and fill
the
distance and spaces
in between.

waiting for love and your
touch, hand in hand and fingers
intertwined in with
feels like, I'm yours and you're mine.

Form: Golden Shovel

Newspaper boats

torrential rainfall
everywhere streams of water
newspaper boats float

changed scenery seen
bran-new waterfalls created
rejuvenates mind

accumulated
knee-deep water on the road
dogs learned to swim

Form: Haiku

Fall sweet fall

Two old brothers at the bar
sat to discuss about, are
very old sellers of coal tar
Aim "Think before drink".

Two old brothers in the hall
they meet each other and recall
the special 'Season of fall'
"Autumn,fall sweet fall"

Form: Kouta

Soul

The
holy
spirit is
inner guidance
itself.

Our
body
emotions
and mind are one
soul.

Soul
transcends
an active
and positive
state.

Form: Lanturne

Suffice smile

Dark spell, in love above and beyond
As the skyline meets the sky beyond
They went the extra mile
Didn't gain suffice smile
As usual they could not respond

Form: Limerick

State of love

Let's meet
eye to eye and
twist together our minds.
Let love blossom and waft its scent
around.
Let's keep
away the clouds
of darkness and always
feel the presence of mind and state
of love.

Form: Mirror Cinquain

Ode to death

If eternal sleep means death and not slumber
But some sleep and ne'er wake up the unknown
fear
Then after a long time, what's a long number?
Mind daunt to hear such news,it stretches an ear

If a person gets endless sleep gets relief
So when God's last call reaches us, why'd others
weep?
Why do someone close to that one undergo
grief?
Why do the eyes get wet and die out the sleep?

You,the former soul protects your dead body
We do not know the truth but this is a fact
You, the former soul change your embody
You can pass through the keyhole and act and
react

Form: Pindaric Ode

I found you

Into the core of my heart
saved the picture of you.
I wish never to apart
so always try to be true.

I found you…

In the darkest part
to start life anew.
If you are going to depart
think how I'll live without you.

Form: Puente

Spaces between us

Spaces
between us defuse thirst for love
is like a fish that longs
for a little
water

Some dreams
come true while others crumble like
a beach castle destroyed
by a strong wave
with ease

Form: Reverse Cinquain

Incomparable

on a moonlit night
the moon peeks out at the stars
fabulous shy moon

moon shines and reflects
image glorifies nature
a mirrored image

the scars on her face
he compares to the moon
incomparable

Form: Senryu

Mi amor

A Crimson
sweet-scented red rose
is offered.
Mi amor,
my divine magical love
accept lovingly.

Form: Shadorma

No control over the mind

No control over the mind

Naive mind hustle,bustle and twirl
As the dust is blown in a wind whirl

Still tries to understand the situation
From birth to birth, the mind seeks destination
Although contented in imagination
Struggles to get close in origination

Naive mind is like the door latch tirl
Works smoothly,if two drops of oil swirl

No control over the mind

Form: symetrelle

Tears swallowed

eyes filled to the brim
lips tremble and heart crumble
emotional mind
tears swallowed in silence
unable to control that

Form: Tanka

Friend

Friend
can be
the best and
worst part of life.
A friend is someone with whom we feel strong.
Theirs emotional connection supports.
A friend builds a
life as faith
builds a
path.
Friend
has the
power to
make you happy.
I believe friendship is the greatest gift.

Form: Triple Tetractys

The crazy minds

a shower of love
a spark of flame shone in eyes
the crazy minds matched

a shower of love
rain bloomed mind into a rose
a passionate love

a spark of flame shone
somewhere far away in hearts
mysterious love

the crazy minds matched
fell in love,loved and promised
unforgettable love

Form: Troiku

You promised

A dream in bright daylight
You met me in lover's paradise
You promised to see me again tonight

Lightened the burden of the mind
My choice is wise
A dream in bright daylight

You are kind
Your picture I picturise
You promised to see me again tonight

Our casette of love, I rewind
Why are we both idolise?
A dream in bright daylight

I miss the goal, you remind
Every meet with you energise
You promised to see me again tonight

Answers to questions, I find
Our love story, i revise
A dream in bright daylight
You promised to see me again tonight

Form: Villanelle

www.ingramcontent.com/pod-product-compliance
Lightning Source LLC
LaVergne TN
LVHW021358200726
843509LV00014B/2911